First Facts®

Christmas around the World

Christmas in the PHILIPPINES

by Cheryl L. Enderlein

CAPSTONE PRESS
a capstone imprint

First Facts are published by Capstone Press,
1710 Roe Crest Drive, North Mankato, Minnesota 56003
www.capstonepub.com

Library of Congress Cataloging-in-Publication Data
Enderlein, Cheryl L.
Christmas in the Philippines / by Cheryl L. Enderlein.
p. cm. — (First facts. Christmas around the world)
Includes bibliographical references and index.
Summary: "Describes the customs, songs, foods, and activities associated with the celebration of
Christmas in the Philippines"—Provided by publisher.
ISBN 978-1-62065-139-1 (library binding)
ISBN 978-1-4765-1063-7 (eBook PDF)
1. Christmas—Philippines—Juvenile literature. 2. Philppines—Social life and customs—Juvenile
literature. I. Title.

GT4987.76.E63 2013
394.266309599—dc23

2012026462

Editorial Credits
Christine Peterson, editor; Ted Williams, designer; Eric Gohl, media researcher; Kathy McColley,
production specialist

Photo Credits
AP Images: Aaron Favila, cover, 17; BigStockPhoto.com: tonyoquias, 6; Capstone Studio: Karon
Dubke, 21; Getty Images: AFP/Ted Aljibe, 20; Newscom: Design Pics, 14, EPA/Dennis M.
Sabangan, 1, EPA/Francis R. Malasig, 9, Getty Images/AFP/Jay Directo, 10, Getty Images/AFP/
Luis Liwanag, 13, Getty Images/AFP/Romeo Gacad, 5; Wikipedia: Kguirnela, 18

Design Elements: Shutterstock

Printed in China
092012   006934LEOS13

TABLE OF CONTENTS

Christmas in the Philippines

Welcome to the Philippines! During Christmas this island country is called the "Land of **Fiestas**." Filipinos say their Christmas celebrations are the longest and most joyful in the world. In this country Christmas celebrations begin December 16. The festivities end the first Sunday in January. This day is known as the "Feast of the **Three Kings**."

fiesta—a holiday or religious festival, especially in Spanish-speaking countries
Three Kings—three kings who are believed to have followed a star to find Jesus in Bethlehem

The map shows the location of the Philippines, labeled "Philippines."

How to Say It!

In the Philippines, people say *"Maligayang Pasko"* (mah-lee-GAH-yang pahs-KOH). This phrase means "Merry Christmas."

CHRISTMAS FACT!

It is believed shepherds and kings followed a bright star to find Jesus.

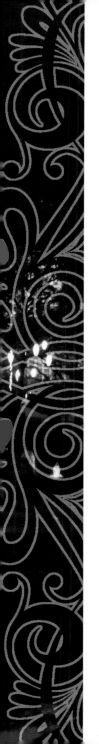

The First Christmas

Christians celebrate the birth of **Jesus** on Christmas. Long ago Jesus' parents, Mary and Joseph, went to Bethlehem. But this town in the Middle East was very crowded. Mary was going to have a baby, but they had no place to stay. So they spent the night in a stable, where Jesus was born. Shepherds and kings came to the stable to celebrate his birth.

Christian—a person who follows a religion based on the teachings of Jesus
Jesus—the founder of the Christian religion

Christmas Celebrations

Church bells mark the start of Christmas in the Philippines. On December 16 bells ring at 4:00 in the morning. People get up and go to church. They go to church every day for the next nine days.

On Christmas Eve, people go to midnight mass. When church is over, people gather for *Noche Buena* (NOH-chay BWAY-nuh). This celebration lasts all night and includes food, music, and gifts.

CHRISTMAS FACT!

The December 16 mass is called *Misa de Gallo* (MEE-suh deh GAHL-yoh). This name means "Mass of the Rooster."

9

CHRISTMAS FACT!
Filipinos begin making parols two or three months before Christmas.

10

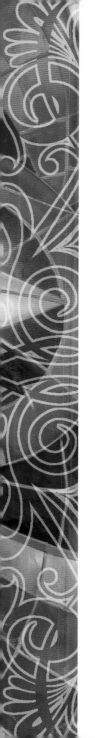

Christmas Symbols

Brightly colored *parols* fill streets and homes in the Philippines during Christmas. A parol is a five-pointed star that is often placed inside a circle. Parols remind people of the star the Three Kings followed to find Jesus. Parols are usually made from **bamboo** and bright paper. Candles or other lights are placed inside parols.

bamboo—a tropical grass with a hard, hollow stem

Christmas Decorations

Parols are popular, but Filipinos also decorate Christmas trees. Few **evergreens** grow in the Philippines. Many people use fake trees. Some use palm tree branches. Others make trees from twigs and cardboard.

People decorate their trees with lights and ornaments. Ornaments are often made from fruit, shells, and bamboo.

evergreen—a tree or bush that has green needles all year long

CHRISTMAS FACT!

Santa Claus is not a big part of Christmas in the Philippines. Children there know about Santa, but he does not bring presents.

Lolo and Lola

Grandparents play a special role in Filipino Christmas celebrations.
In the Philippines they are called *Lolo* (grandfather) and *Lola* (grandmother).
During a family's holiday feast, Lolo and Lola give gifts to their grandchildren. They usually have the kids play games to get their gifts. In one game grandparents throw gold coins into the air. The children then rush in to get the money.

Christmas Presents

Christmas gifts in the Philippines are simple and useful. Many people get new clothes that they wear to midnight mass. During the Noche Buena celebration, people go house to house visiting family. Children usually get a small gift at each house. Gifts might be toys, money, or candy.

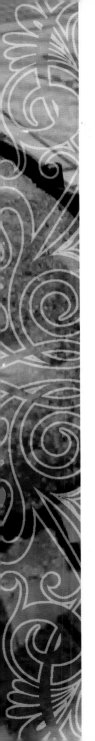

Christmas Food

Food covers family tables during Christmas feasts in the Philippines. During Noche Buena, at least 15 different foods are served. People enjoy chicken and rice soup. They eat spring rolls stuffed with meat and vegetables. A pancake made with rice flour is a favorite dessert. The pancake, called *bibingka* (bee-BING-kah), is cooked with milk, cheese, and duck eggs. It is served with coconut and brown sugar.

Christmas Songs

Young and old join together to sing Christmas songs in the Philippines. People sing every night, beginning December 16. Groups of children called *cumbancheros* (kum-ban-CHAY-rohs) sing as they go house to house. Some play musical instruments.

Hands-On:
MAKE A PAROL

People in the Philippines decorate their homes with brightly colored stars called parols. Make your own parol to add some color to your holiday home.

What You Need

- scissors
- cereal box
- glue

- tissue paper
- strips of ribbon
- paper plate (optional)

What You Do

1. With an adult's help, cut the cereal box into five strips. Each strip should be 1 inch (2.5 centimeters) wide and 15 inches (38 cm) long.
2. Glue two strips together at one end to form a flat V shape. Repeat with two other strips.
3. Place one V so that its open end faces to the right. Overlap the first V with the second V, so that the bottom ends connect. The point of the second V will form the top of your star. Use the last strip to connect the open ends. Glue all ends together.
4. Spread a thin layer of glue around your star's frame. Place a piece of tissue paper over the star. Let dry and repeat on the other side. When dry, trim off extra paper.
5. Glue ribbon strips to the star's ends. You can also glue your parol to a paper plate before hanging it.

GLOSSARY

bamboo (bam-BOO)—a tropical grass with a hard, hollow stem

Christian (KRIS-chuhn)—a person who follows a religion based on the teachings of Jesus

evergreen (E-vuhr-green)—a tree or bush that has green needles all year long

fiesta (fee-ESS-tuh)—a holiday or religious festival in Spanish-speaking countries

Jesus (JEE-zuhss)—founder of the Christian religion

Three Kings (THREE KINGS)—three kings who are said to have followed a star to find Jesus in Bethlehem

Read More

Franchino, Vicky. *It's Cool to Learn about Countries: Philippines.* Social Studies Explorer. Ann Arbor, Mich.: Cherry Lake Pub., 2010.

Kalman, Bobbie. *Spotlight on the Philippines.* Spotlight on My Country. New York: Crabtree Pub. Co., 2011.

Trunkhill, Brenda. *Christmas around the World.* St. Louis: Concordia Publishing House, 2009.

Internet Sites

FactHound offers a safe, fun way to find Internet sites related to this book. All of the sites on FactHound have been researched by our staff.

Here's all you do:

Visit *www.facthound.com*

Type in this code: 9781620651391

Super-cool stuff!

Check out projects, games and lots more at
www.capstonekids.com

Index